Christmas
Around the World

Christmas in Norway

by Kristin Thoennes

Consultant:
Hilde Haaland Kramer
Coordinator of International Education
Royal Norwegian Consulate General

Hilltop Books
an Imprint of Franklin Watts
A Division of Grolier Publishing
New York   London   Hong Kong   Sydney
Danbury, Connecticut

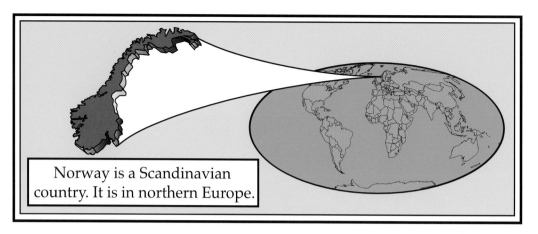

Norway is a Scandinavian country. It is in northern Europe.

Hilltop Books
http://publishing.grolier.com
Copyright © 1999 by Capstone Press. All rights reserved.
Published simultaneously in Canada. Printed in the United States of America.
No part of this book may be reproduced without written permission from the publisher.
The publisher takes no responsibility for the use of any of the materials or methods
described in this book, nor for the products thereof.

Library of Congress Cataloging-in-Publication Data
Thoennes, Kristin.
    Christmas in Norway/by Kristin Thoennes.
        p. cm.—(Christmas around the world)
    Includes bibliographical references and index.
    Summary: An overview of the symbols, celebrations, decorations, food, and songs that are part of
Christmas in Norway.
    ISBN 0-7368-0091-3
    1. Christmas—Norway—Juvenile literature. 2. Norway—Social life and customs—Juvenile literature.
[1. Christmas—Norway. 2. Norway—Social life and customs. 3. Holidays.]
    I. Title. II. Series.
    GT4887.59.T56 1999
    394.2663'09481—dc21   98-16027
                                                                      CIP
                                                                      AC

Editorial Credits
Michelle L. Norstad, editor; James Franklin, cover designer and illustrator; Sheri Gosewisch,
  photo researcher
Photo Credits
Ingrid Marn Wood, 12
Mittet Foto, 4, 18
Photri-Microstock, 8
Trip Photo Library, cover, 10, 14, 16, 20
Unicorn Stock Photos/Gerry Schnieders, 6

Table of Contents

Christmas in Norway

Christmas is a holiday that people celebrate around the world. People celebrate holidays by doing something enjoyable. People in different countries celebrate Christmas in different ways.

Norway is a country in an area of northern Europe called Scandinavia. People from Norway are Norwegians. They speak the Norwegian language. Their Christmas greeting is God Jul (GOH YUHL). It means Good Christmas.

Norwegians celebrate Christmas on December 24. This is Christmas Eve. But Norwegians begin preparing for the Christmas season four Sundays before Christmas. The Christmas season lasts until January 13 in Norway.

The weather in Norway during the Christmas season is usually snowy. It is often dark in Norway at this time. The sun shines for only a few hours each day.

The weather in Norway during the Christmas season is snowy.

The First Christmas

Christmas is a celebration of Jesus Christ's birthday. Many people who celebrate Christmas are Christians. Christians follow the teachings of Jesus Christ.

Jesus' parents traveled to Bethlehem before he was born. Their names were Mary and Joseph. They tried to find a room at an inn. Mary and Joseph could not find a room.

Mary and Joseph had to stay in a building for animals called a stable. Jesus was born in the stable. His first bed was a manger. A manger is a food box for animals. Mary and Joseph put straw in the manger. The straw kept Jesus warm.

Three kings followed a bright star the night Jesus was born. The star led them to Jesus. The kings brought gifts for him.

Mary and Joseph had to stay in a stable.

Juleneks

The julenek (YUH-le-nek) is a symbol of Christmas in Norway. A julenek is stalks of oats tied to a pole. The poles are often tree branches. People hang juleneks as symbols of hope for good farming.

Long ago, Norwegians put juleneks outside on Christmas Eve. It was good luck if birds ate from the juleneks.

Norwegian families in farming areas still put out juleneks. People clear away a circle of snow below each julenek. They believe the birds dance in the circle before eating.

Norwegians living in cities also put out juleneks. People sometimes put the juleneks in front of their homes. People in apartments hang juleneks on outdoor railings.

A julenek is a symbol of Christmas in Norway.

Decorations

Most Norwegians have Christmas trees. They decorate them with glass balls, tinsel, and strings of lights or candles. Tinsel is a thin, shiny piece of paper or metal. Some trees have pinecones, stars, and birds as decorations. Strings of small Norwegian flags also are common. Many Norwegians put lighted stars on top of their trees.

Norwegians decorate their homes for the Christmas season. Some of these decorations are found in nature. Branches, pinecones, moss, and straw are common. People sometimes put these decorations in bowls or baskets.

Many Norwegians make their own decorations. Heart-shaped baskets are popular. Norwegian children usually make paper chains. The chains are long and colorful. Families often put them on Christmas trees.

Norwegians decorate Christmas trees with glass balls, tinsel, and strings of lights or candles.

Christmas Celebrations

Most Norwegians celebrate Saint Lucia Day on December 13. Saint Lucia was a Christian who helped others. She often brought food to the hungry.

In the past, people celebrated Saint Lucia Day in their homes. The oldest daughter woke early on Saint Lucia Day. She dressed in a long, white gown with a red belt. The daughter also wore a crown with candles on her head. She took food to her family. This is how Norwegians remembered Saint Lucia.

Today, Norwegians mostly celebrate Saint Lucia Day in schools and other public places. A girl dressed as Saint Lucia leads a procession. Girls and boys follow her through the building.

Many Norwegians celebrate Little Christmas Eve on December 23. Parents bring in Christmas trees while the children sleep. The children see the decorated trees in the morning. The children sometimes find presents under the trees.

On Saint Lucia Day, a girl in a long, white gown leads a procession.

Julenissen

Long ago, many Norwegians believed in the nisse (NI-se). He was an elf-like spirit. The nisse protected farms if people did their work well. He would play tricks if people did work poorly.

People left bowls of porridge for the nisse on Christmas Eve. They believed this would please the nisse. Today, some people still leave a bowl of porridge for the nisse.

Most Norwegian children believe in Julenissen (YUH-le-ni-sen). Julenissen is a mix of the nisse and Santa Claus. He has a long, white beard and wears a red cap. Julenissen brings presents to children's homes. He carries the presents in a sack on his back.

Julenissen always says the same thing when he arrives. He asks if there are any good children there. Children sometimes hug him when he comes.

Julenissen brings toys to children's homes.

Christmas Presents

Both Christian and non-Christian people give presents at Christmas time. But giving presents reminds Christians of the gifts the three kings brought to Jesus.

Norwegian families give presents in different ways. Some parents place gifts under Christmas trees. Others tie small presents to the lower branches.

Other Norwegian families say Julenissen brings all the gifts. He carries them in a sack. Julenissen brings something for everyone in the family.

Children in Norway receive many types of presents. Some may receive toys, books, and games. Others may receive skis, sleds, or skates.

Warm clothing is another kind of gift. Adults and children may give mittens, hats, or scarves. They may also give stockings or sweaters.

Children in Norway receive many types of presents.

Holiday Foods

Pork is the most common Christmas Eve meal in Norway. Pork is the meat from a pig. Many Norwegians eat boiled potatoes with pork. They also eat sweet and sour cabbage. Cabbage is a leafy vegetable with green or purple leaves.

Lutefisk (LOO-te-fisk) also is common. Lutefisk is codfish. People soak the cod in a liquid called lye. This flavors and preserves the fish. Then they bake it.

Most Norwegians like julekake (YUH-le-kah-ke) at Christmas time. Julekake is a sweet bread with raisins. Many Norwegians spread butter on the bread.

Lefse (LEF-se) is another Christmas treat in Norway. Lefse is a flat, sweetened bread. Norwegians usually eat lefse with butter and sugar.

Cookies are popular Christmas treats in Norway. Many people bake several different kinds of cookies. Norwegians offer these cookies to guests.

Cookies are popular Christmas treats in Norway.

Christmas Songs

Many families in Norway sing together during the Christmas season. They join hands and walk around their Christmas tree. They sing as they circle the tree. Small families hold stuffed animals and dolls between them. This makes the circle large enough to reach around the tree.

Norwegians also may sing around trees in other places. They may sing in churches or at work. Norwegians sometimes form many rings around trees. Norwegians do this when there are many singers. Each ring walks in a different direction from the rings next to it.

Church bells ring throughout Norway at 5 p.m. on December 24. They ring fast for several minutes. This lets Norwegians know Christmas Eve is beginning.

Many Norwegian families sing as they walk around their Christmas tree.

Hands on: Make a Julenek

Norwegians make a treat for birds called a julenek. You can make your own julenek.

What You Need

A 36-inch-long (91-centimeter-long) branch
Many stalks of grain
String
Brightly colored ribbon

What You Do

1. Surround the branch with stalks of grain.
2. Tie the string around the whole bunch. Make sure to tie it tightly.
3. Tie the ribbon over the string as a decoration.
4. Dig a hole in the ground about five inches (12.7 centimeters) deep.
5. Stick the branch into the hole.
6. Fill the hole with dirt. Pack it around the branch.
7. Watch the birds eat your julenek.

Words to Know

cabbage (KAB-ij)—a leafy vegetable with green or purple leaves

Christian (KRISS-chuhn)—a person who follows the teachings of Jesus Christ

God Jul (GOH YUHL)—Norwegian Christmas greeting meaning Good Christmas

julekake (YUH-le-kah-ke)—Norwegian sweet bread with raisins

julenek (YUH-le-nek)—stalks of oats tied to a pole

Julenissen (YUH-le-ni-sen)—the Christmas person in Norway; Julenissen brings gifts for people.

lefse (LEF-se)—a flat, sweetened bread often eaten with butter and sugar

lutefisk (LOO-te-feesk)—codfish soaked in lye and baked

manger (MAYN-jur)—a food box for animals

pork (PORK)—the meat from a pig

stable (STAY-buhl)—a building for animals

tinsel (TIN-suhl)—a thin, shiny piece of paper or metal

Read More

Kennedy, Pamela. *A Christmas Celebration: Traditions and Customs from Around the World.* Nashville: Ideals Children's Books, 1992.

Lankford, Mary. *Christmas Around the World.* New York: Morrow Junior Books, 1995.

Useful Addresses and Internet Sites

Royal Norwegian Consulate General
825 Third Avenue
New York, NY 10022

Sons of Norway International Headquarters
1455 West Lake Street
Minneapolis, MN 55405

Christmas around the World
http://www.santas.net/aroundtheworld.htm
Christmas.com
http://www.christmas.com
Norwegian Christmas
http://www.norway.org/xmas/menu.htm

Index